STRANGE
and Amazing Plants

LEVEL  READER

READING LEVEL: **2** GRADES 1 TO 3

Written by Kathryn Knight

Copyright © 2014 Bendon Publishing International, Inc.
All rights reserved. Printed in Haining, Zhejiang, China.

The BENDON name and logo are trademarks of Bendon Publishing International, Inc.
Ashland, OH 44805 • 1-888-5-BENDON
bendonpub.com

Taxodium distichum
(bald cypress) of the southeastern United States

Strange and Amazing

• •

Plants are amazing life forms. With just water, air, sunlight, and soil, they grow into a variety of shapes, colors, and sizes. Plants survive in all kinds of environments, from cold, snowy mountains, to dry deserts, to murky swamplands.

Most new plants start out as seeds. Seeds can be so small, they look like dust. The largest seeds belong to the coconut family. Some can weigh 35 pounds! Seeds are often enclosed in a fruit. The granddaddy of all fruits is the giant pumpkin. In 2013, the world's largest weighed 2,032 pounds!

Cucurbita maximus

Largest Flower

Flowers of plants are dainty, lovely blossoms—right? Not always! This flower is huge! It can be 3 feet across and weigh 24 pounds! It blooms close to the ground in a rainforest. Bees do not pollinate this giant. Flies do. And what do flies like? The rotting flesh of a corpse (dead body). So this big beauty has a very strong odor to attract flies. Its nickname is the corpse flower.

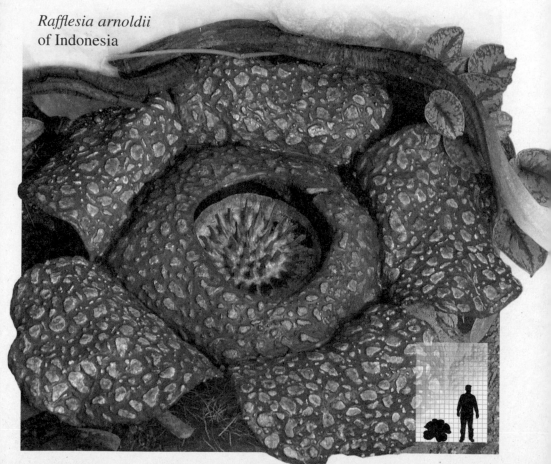

Rafflesia arnoldii
of Indonesia

Big Stinker

Another rotten-smelling giant of the rainforest is this amazing plant, the corpse plant. You will probably hold your nose if you visit one, but flies love it! The tallest bloom on record was over 9 feet tall!

Titan arum of Sumatra

Sequoiadendron giganteum
of California

Gentle Giants

Imagine trees so tall, you could look up, up, up and not see the tops of them! The giant sequoia (seh-**koy**-yah) redwood pines are the largest trees in the world. The tallest are 300 feet tall. The oldest living sequoia may be 3,500 years old. That's a long time to be towering over the earth!

The General Sherman, one of the tallest living things

Desert Guards

Most forms of cactus are fairly short plants. Some grow to be huge. The largest is the cardón (car-**doan**). These giants stand like "armed" guards over the dry land. They are covered with thistle-like spines (ouch!) and can reach 60 feet in height. Amazingly, cardóns don't have deep roots and need little water. Some can grow atop bare rock!

Pachycereus pringlei of the Sonoran Desert, Mexico

Elephant Foot

This odd shrub lives on a dry, desert island off the coast of Africa. It survives by storing water in its thick trunk. It has pretty pink blooms in spring and is called the desert rose. It's also called the bottle tree and elephant foot tree.

Adenium obesum socotranum
of the Socotra Islands
of Yemen, Africa

Elephant Toes

These are not flowers atop stones. They are small, juicy plants called elephant's toes, pebble plants, and living stones. They grow in groups among the smooth rocks of a dry riverbed. They blend in, and animals looking for plant food walk right past them. In autumn, flowers bloom from between the two leaves—or toes!

Lithops of southern Africa

Elephant Ear

Leaves take in light from the sun, and this light helps plants make food. The largest undivided leaves in the world belong to the tropical taro plant. It has leaves that can grow to 9 feet long and 6 feet wide! Its nickname is the elephant ear plant.

Alocasia macrorrhiza, tropical areas of the world

Bambusodae of Asia

Shooting Skyward

Imagine a lawn of grass that grows 18 to 24 inches a day. You could never keep it mowed! That's how fast many bamboo shoots grow. Bamboo is a woody grass, the fastest-growing woody plant in the world. Some bamboos are so fast, you can almost see them grow—as much as 48 inches in a day (2 inches an hour)!

Pueraria lobata of the American South

Creeping Outward

● ●

Vines send out "runners" that trail along the ground and creep up tall objects. The kudzu (**kud**-zoo) vine was brought to southern America from Japan in 1876 and it became "the vine that ate the South." Each runner can grow 12 inches a day, and each plant has many runners. This trailing, climbing creeper can take over entire stretches of ground—trees and all!

Living on Air

Most plants have roots that draw water and food from the soil. Some, however, can almost live on air! Air plants are some of the prettiest plants. They grow on rock or other plants, such as trees. For many, air and rainwater are all they need to live. For some, dirt and leaves collect around their little perch and feed their tiny roots.

Bromeliads of the American and African tropics

Orchids,
tropical areas of the world

There are several types of air plants. Lovely orchids (**or**-kids) come in all colors and shapes. Spanish moss (which is not really a moss) drapes over tree limbs, soaking up air and water.

Spanish moss,
American South

Living on Bugs

Venus was the Roman goddess of love. A pretty little flowering swamp plant is named for her. The ends of its leaves have sweet-smelling "pads" that attract bugs. Bugs just *love* the taste! But as a bug crawls around, it touches hairs on

Dionaea muscipula
of the American swamplands

the pad—and the pad
suddenly closes up into
a cage! The trapped bug
gets mushy over time
and becomes food for
the Venus flytrap.
Love can be cruel!

Sticky Treat

Like the Venus flytrap, the little sundew plant gets its food not from the soil but from bugs. The ends of its leaves sparkle with sweet sticky droplets that look like dew. The perfect treat for a hungry bug! When the bug walks on the leaf, it becomes stuck. The leaf curls around the bug— and it becomes a treat for the plant!

Drosera felix of Venezuela

Nepenthes
coccinea
of Indonesia

Pitcher of Bug Juice

• •

There are several kinds of pitcher plants that live in marshy areas. This lovely plant attracts insects with its color and sweet smell. When a bug steps onto the edge of its cup-shaped leaf, it tumbles right in! The sides are so slippery, the bug cannot climb out. It dissolves in the liquid at the bottom of the pitcher—and is served to the plant.

Desert "Seaweed"

The tree tumbo of Africa is unlike any plant known on Earth. It looks like a clump of seaweed in the desert! This bizarre plant grows slowly, forming only two leaves from a short thick stem that may grow 1 to 5 feet tall. Over time, those two leaves grow and split into thinner straps. By soaking up morning mists, tree tumbos can survive for up to 1,000 years!

Welwitschia mirabilis of the Namib Desert of southern Africa

Macrocystis pyrifera
of coastal waters

Sea "Forest"

One of the most unusual plants on Earth is not a plant at all. Giant kelp, a seaweed, is actually algae (**al**-jee), a plantlike life form. Giant kelp grow in "forests," stretching from the bottom of a seabed to the water's surface, perhaps 140 feet above. Giant kelp can grow 2 feet a day! The thick forests are home to fish and other water animals.

Life on Stilts

Red mangrove trees live in salty, swampy waters. Too much water can harm a plant, so these trees have an amazing way of staying above the water line. They have "prop roots" that are like stilts! These roots form thickets where birds, animals, and water creatures can live.

Rhizophora mangle
of the American
and Asian tropics